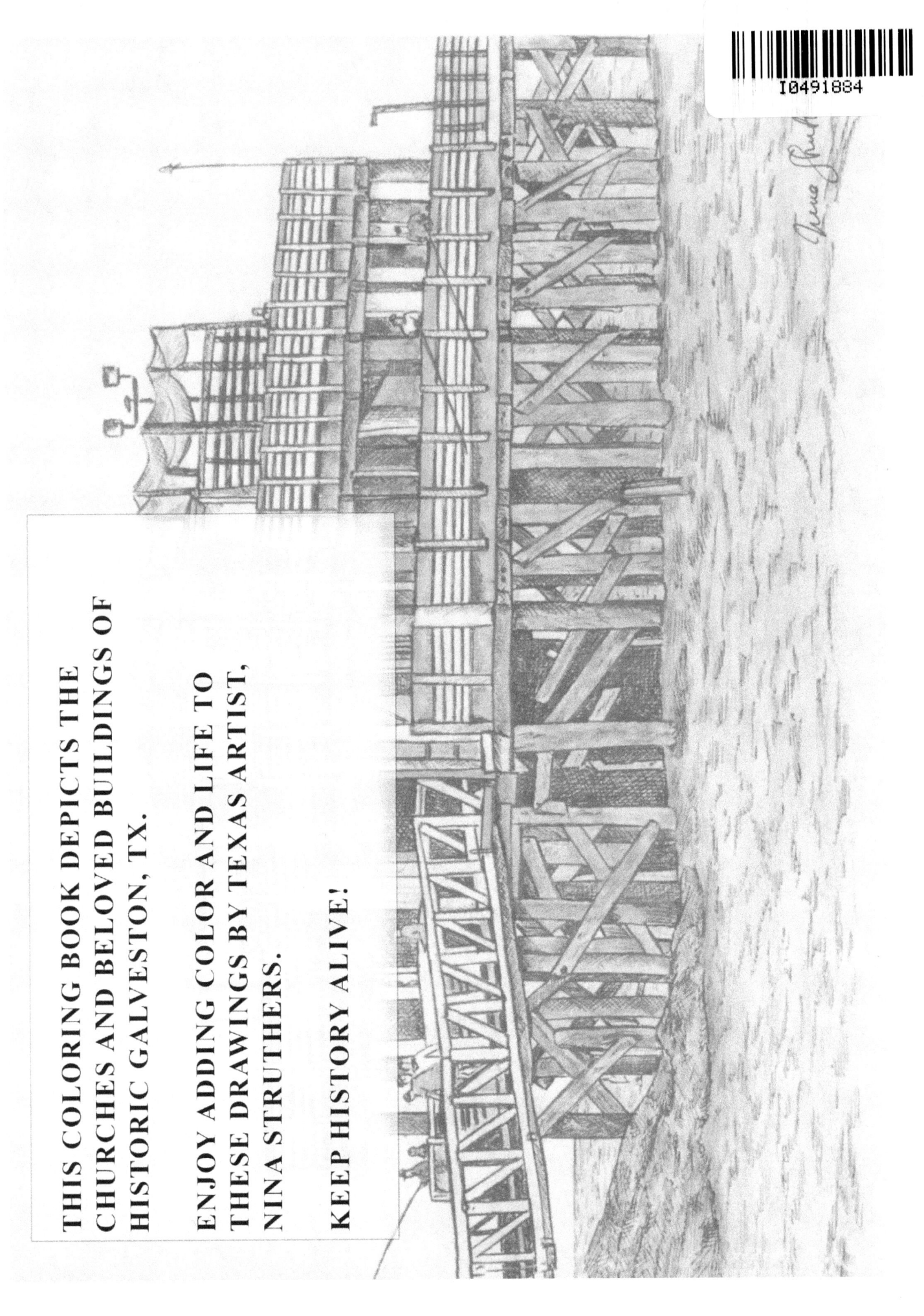

THIS COLORING BOOK DEPICTS THE CHURCHES AND BELOVED BUILDINGS OF HISTORIC GALVESTON, TX.

ENJOY ADDING COLOR AND LIFE TO THESE DRAWINGS BY TEXAS ARTIST, NINA STRUTHERS.

KEEP HISTORY ALIVE!

The Artist recommends that you use watercolor pencils to color these drawings. Markers are good, but watercolor pencils are better.

Prismacolor is a good brand of pencil.

Looking at your watercolor pencils, choose the color you would like for your drawing. Then, color the areas, but do not press too hard. The harder you press the deeper the color you will get.

After coloring your drawing, get a watercolor brush and a jar of clean water. Brush over your colored areas with a damp brush, but make sure your brush isn't dripping wet. You will see that the darker you press with your pencils, the deeper color you will get when you add water. Be Careful Practice on a blank piece of paper before you get started on your drawings.

Enjoy!

Victorians on Post Office Street

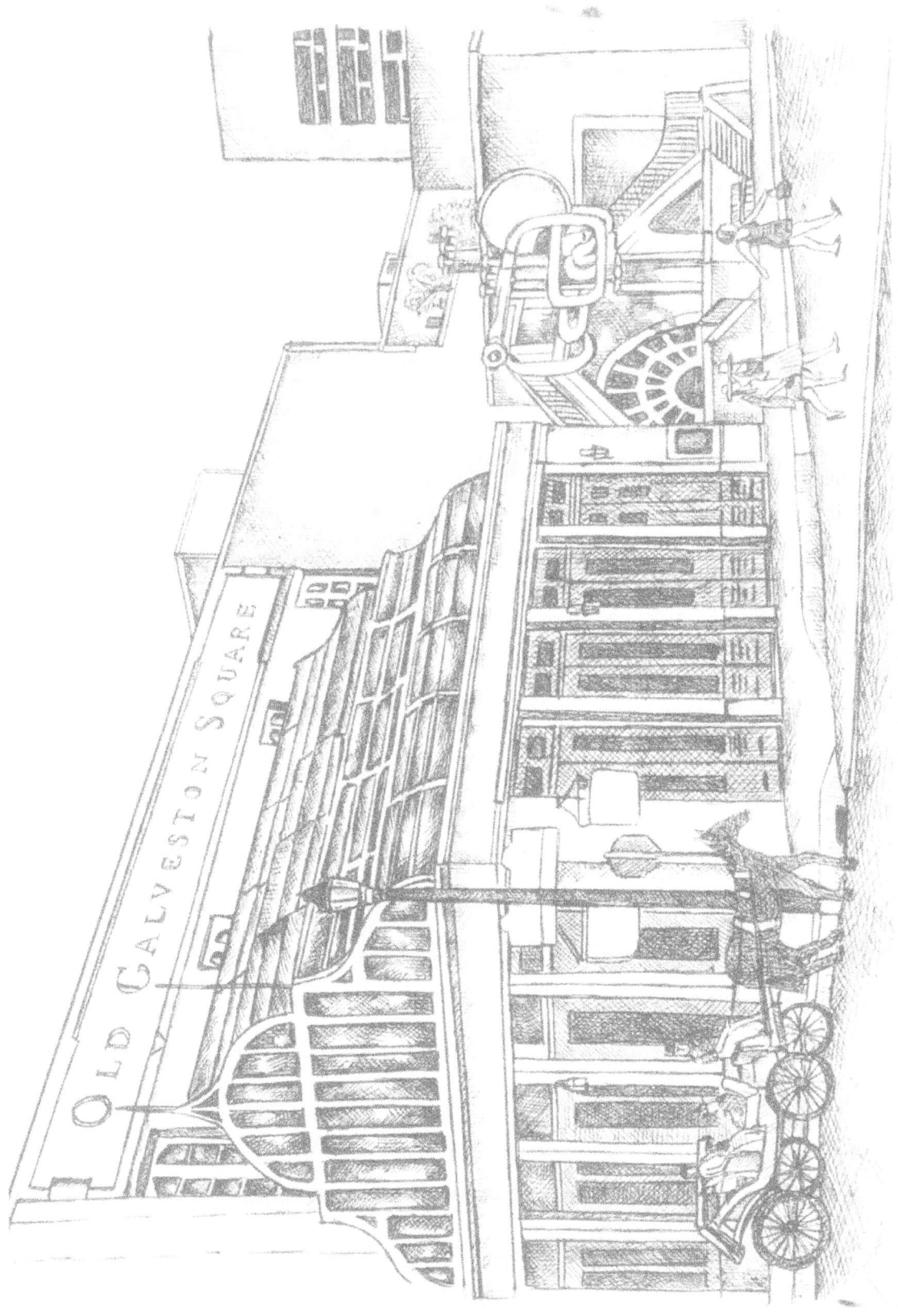

Old Galveston Square

View of The Strand

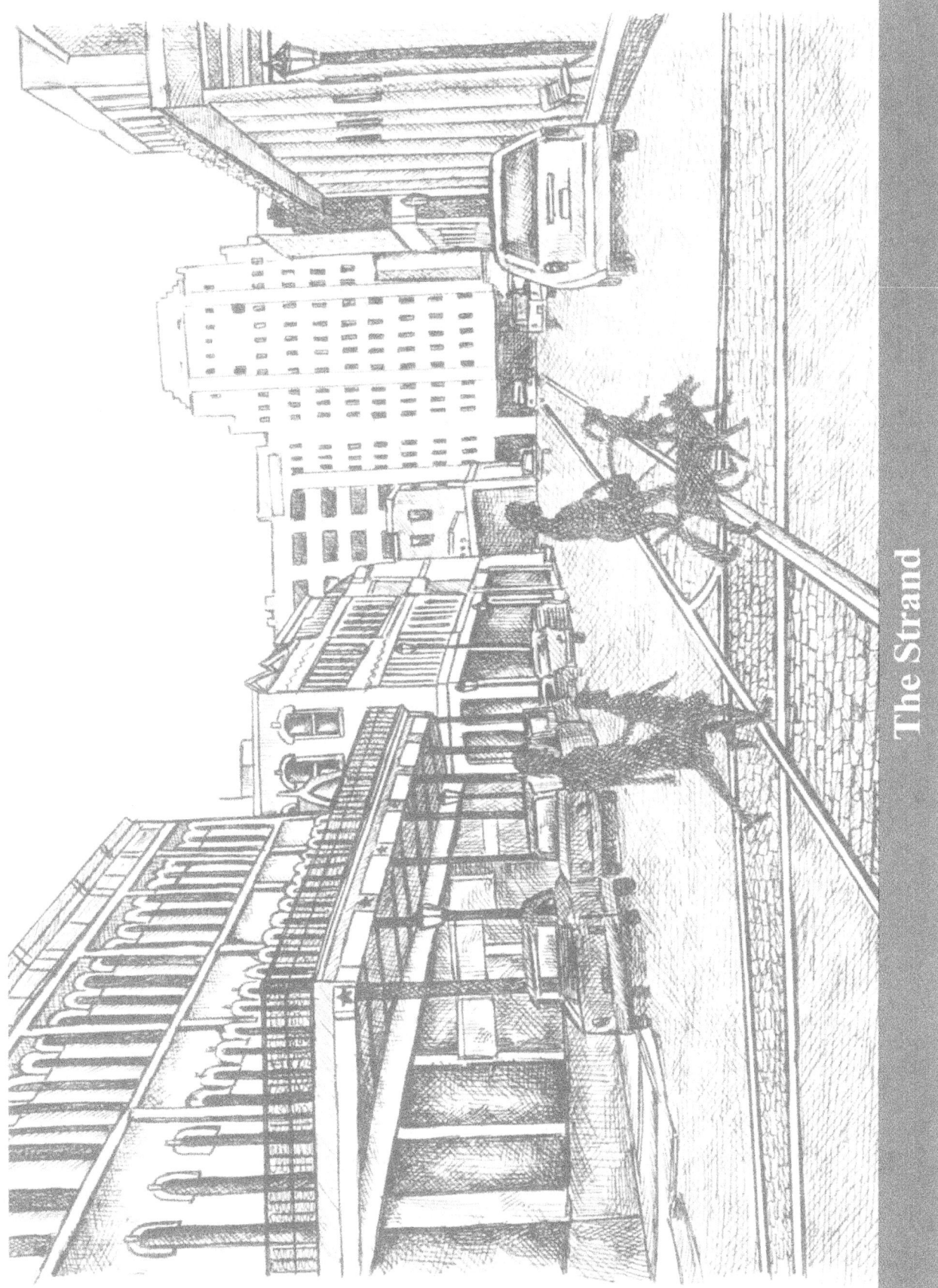

The Strand

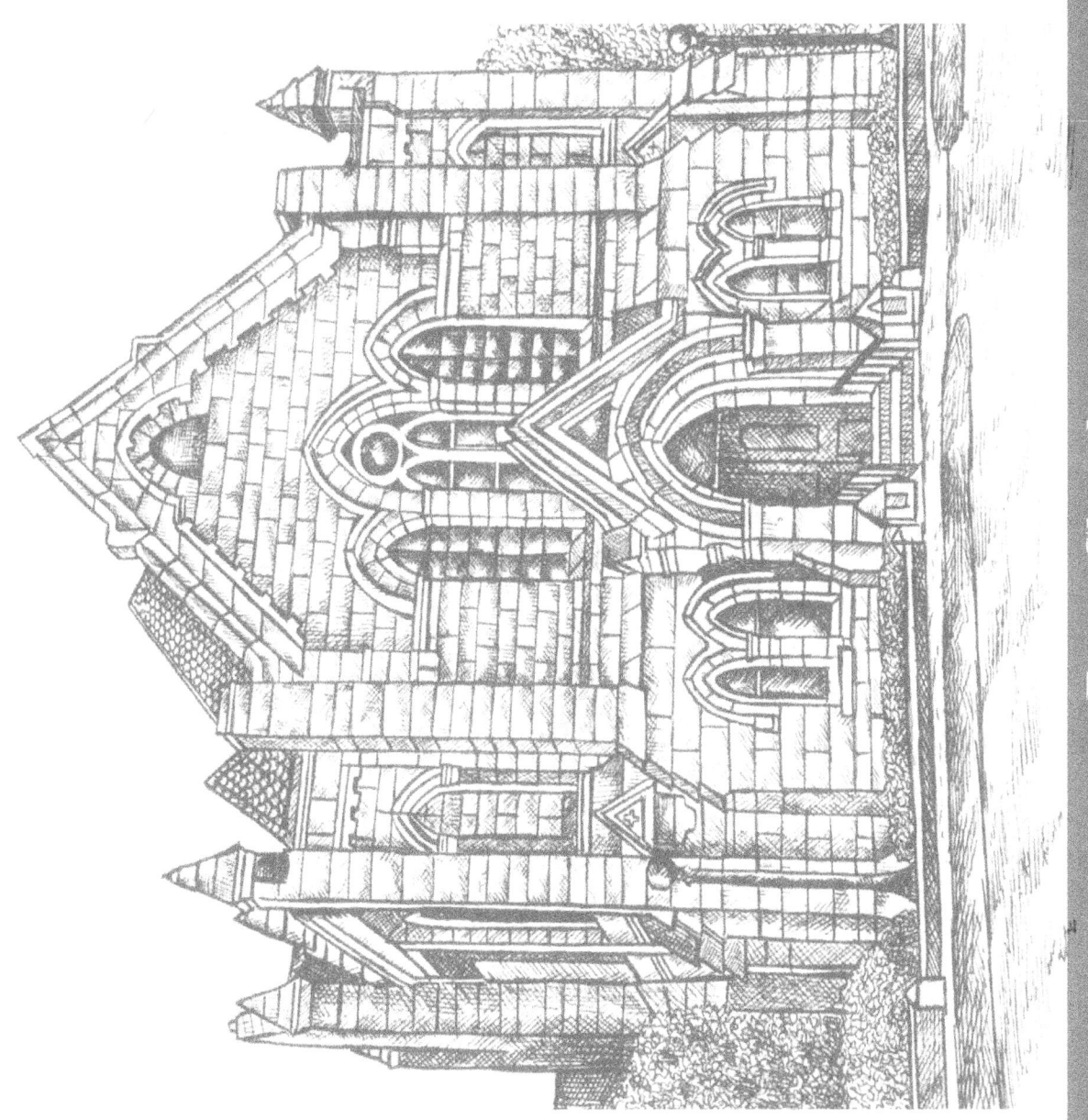

Eaton Chapel

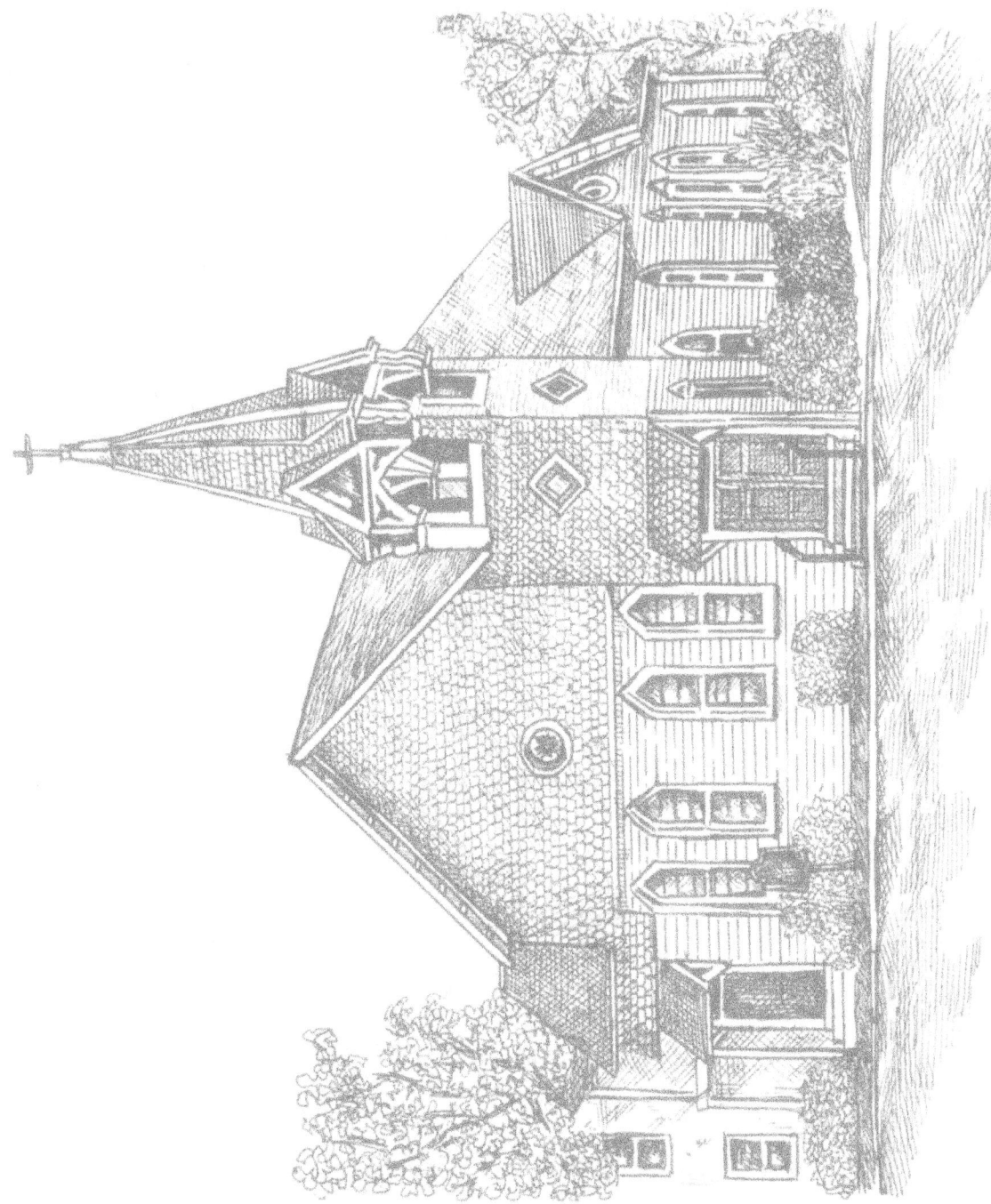

St. Paul's United Methodist Church

The Garten Verein

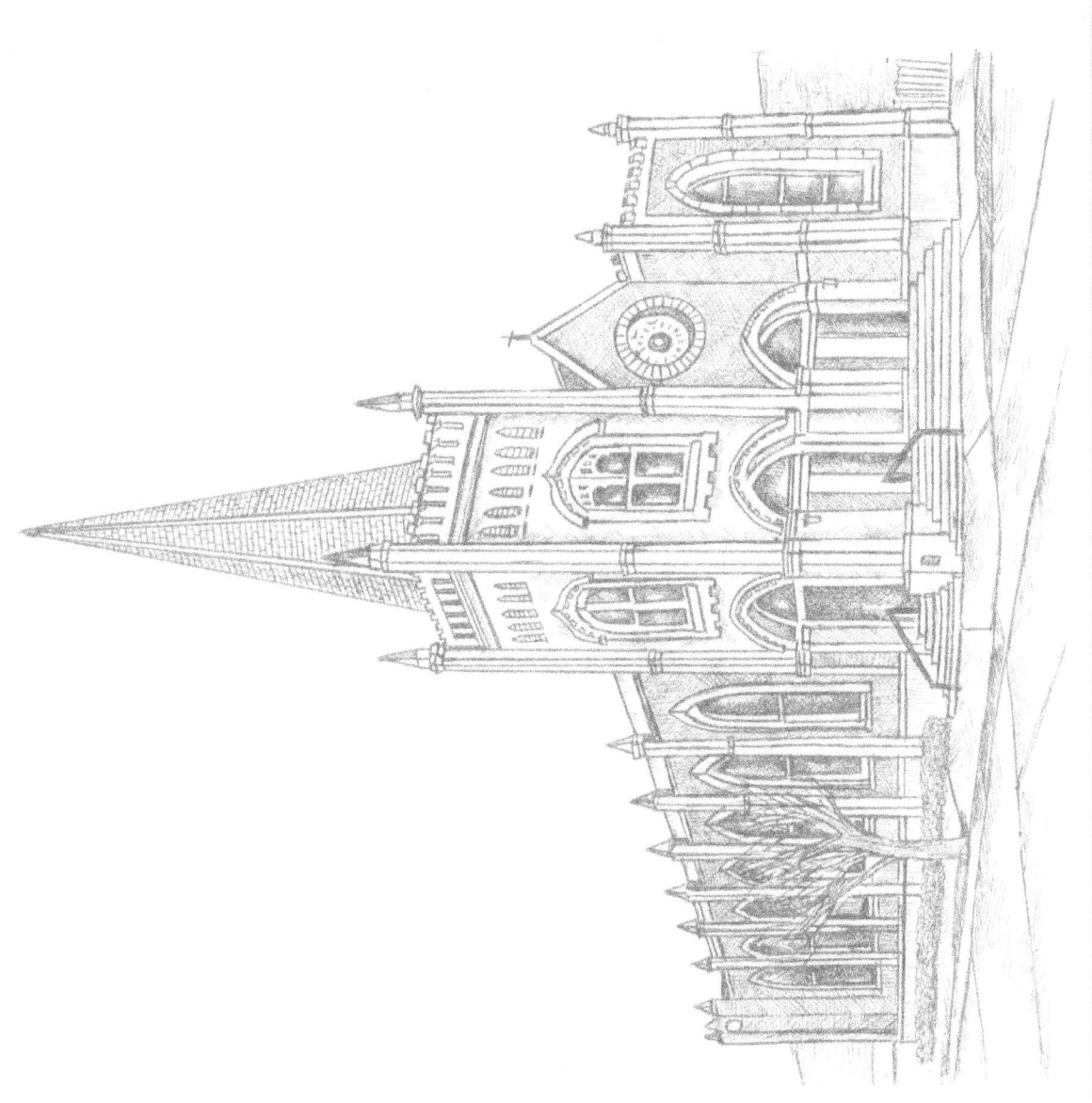

The Lyceum

St. Patrick's Catholic Church

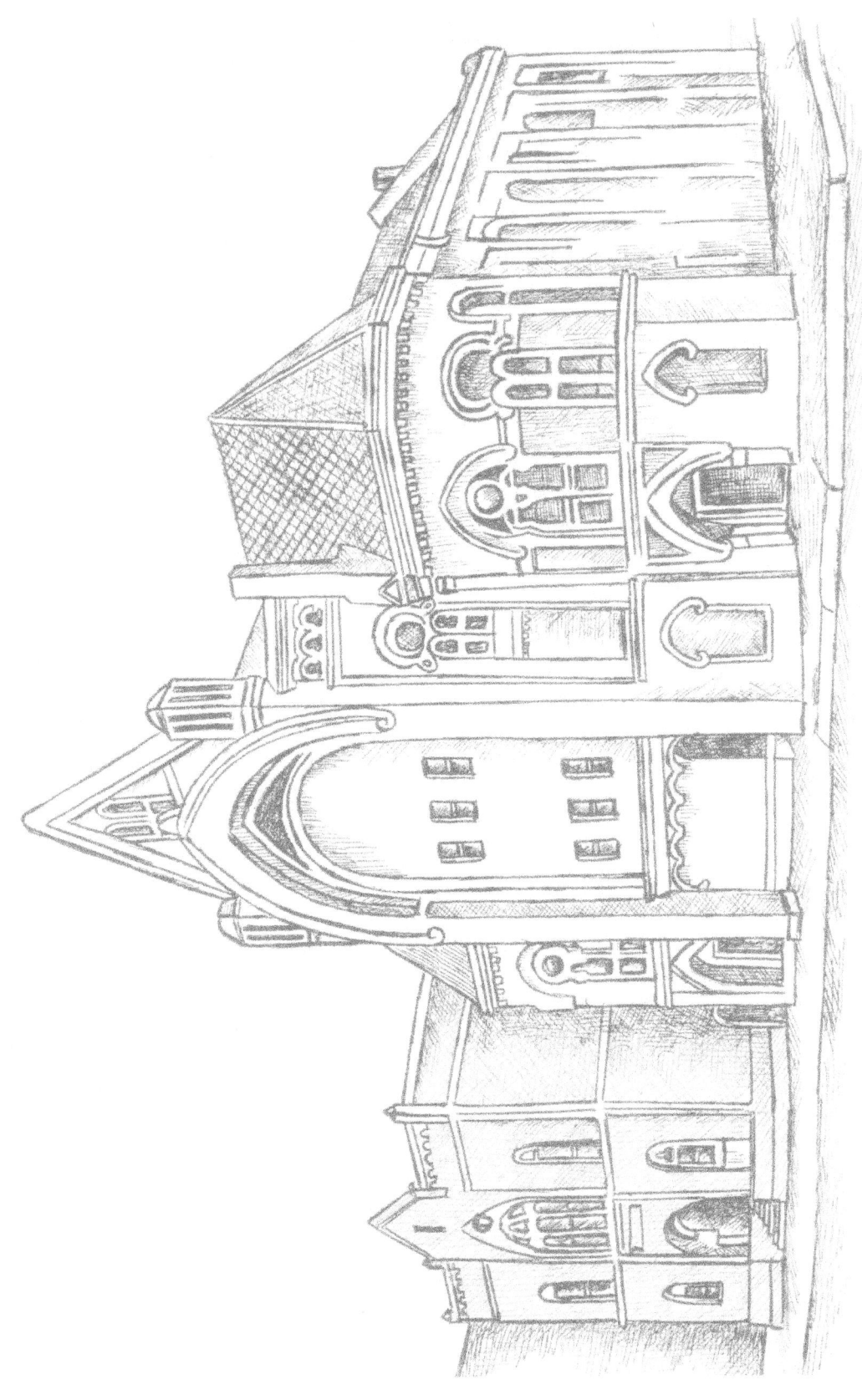

The Galveston Movement

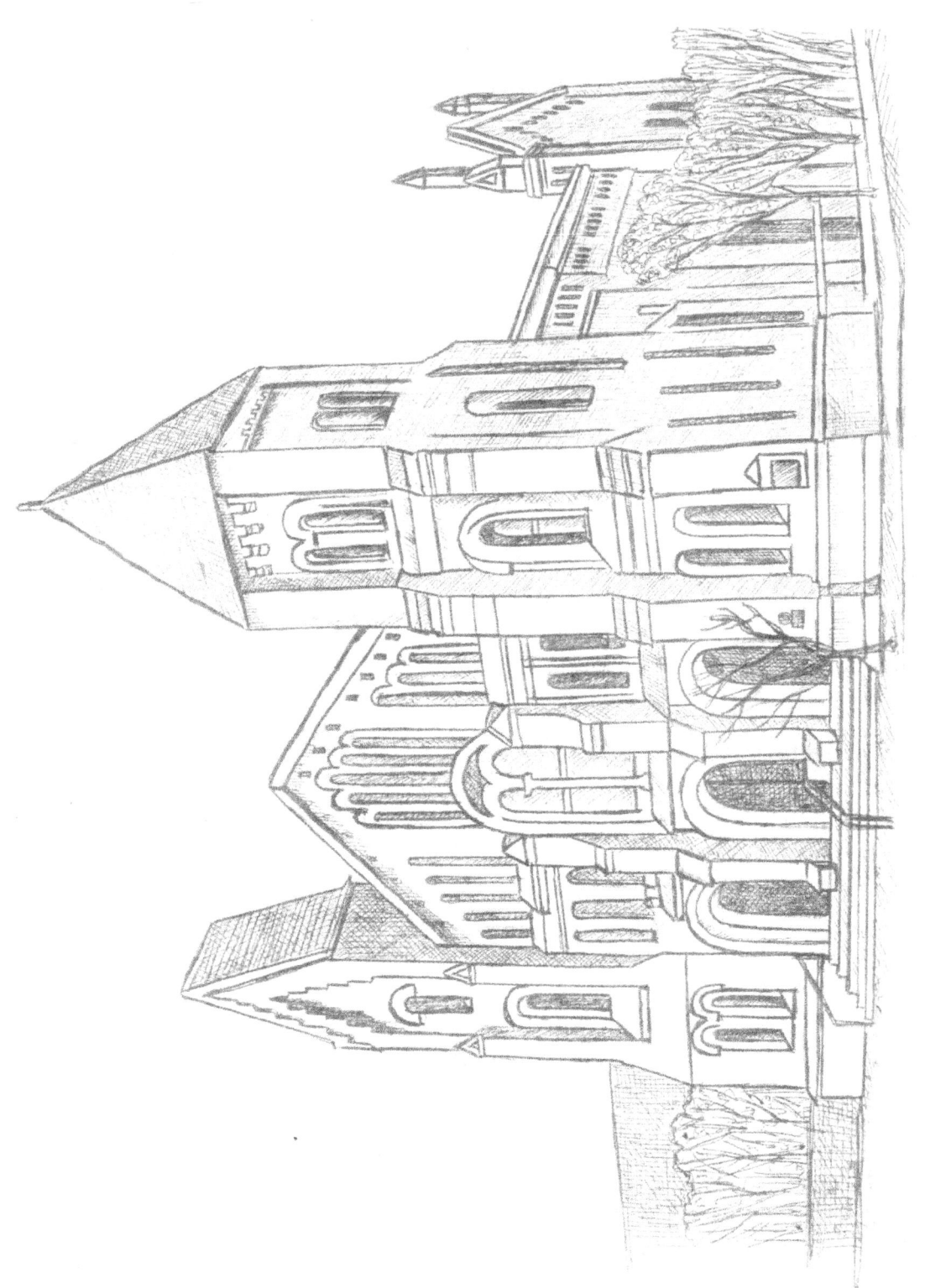

First Presbyterian Church

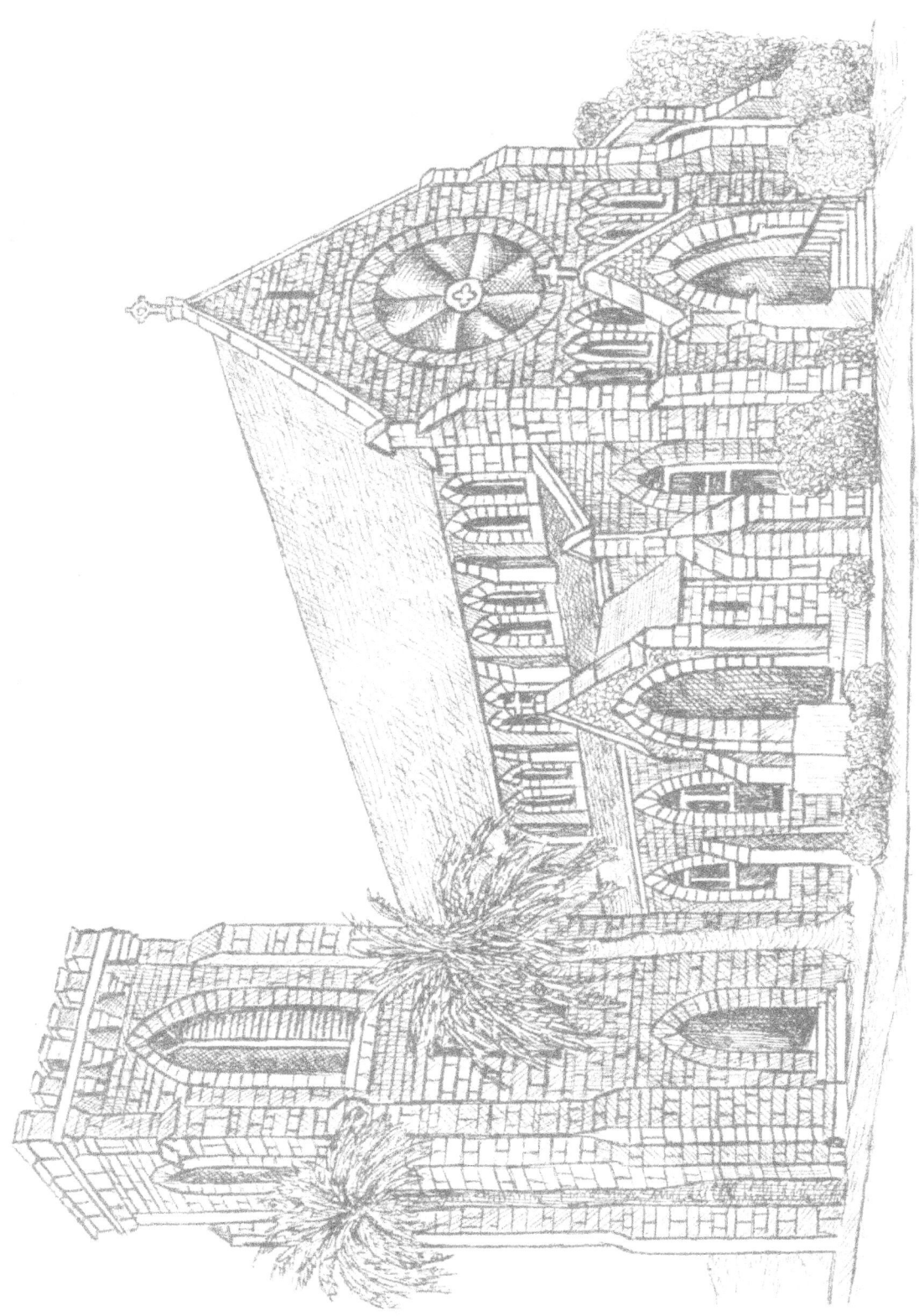

Grace Episcopal Church

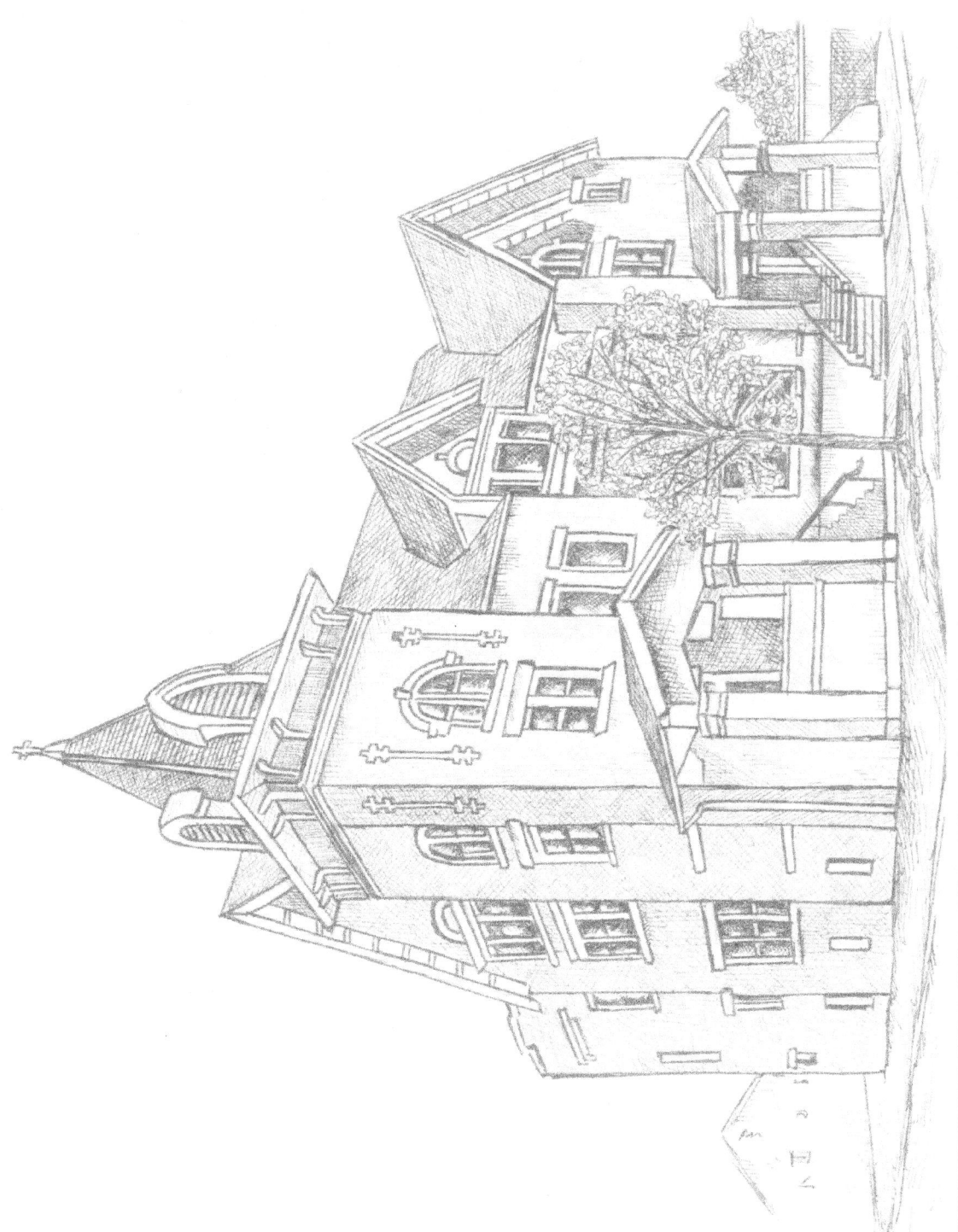

Wesley Tabernacle United Methodist Church

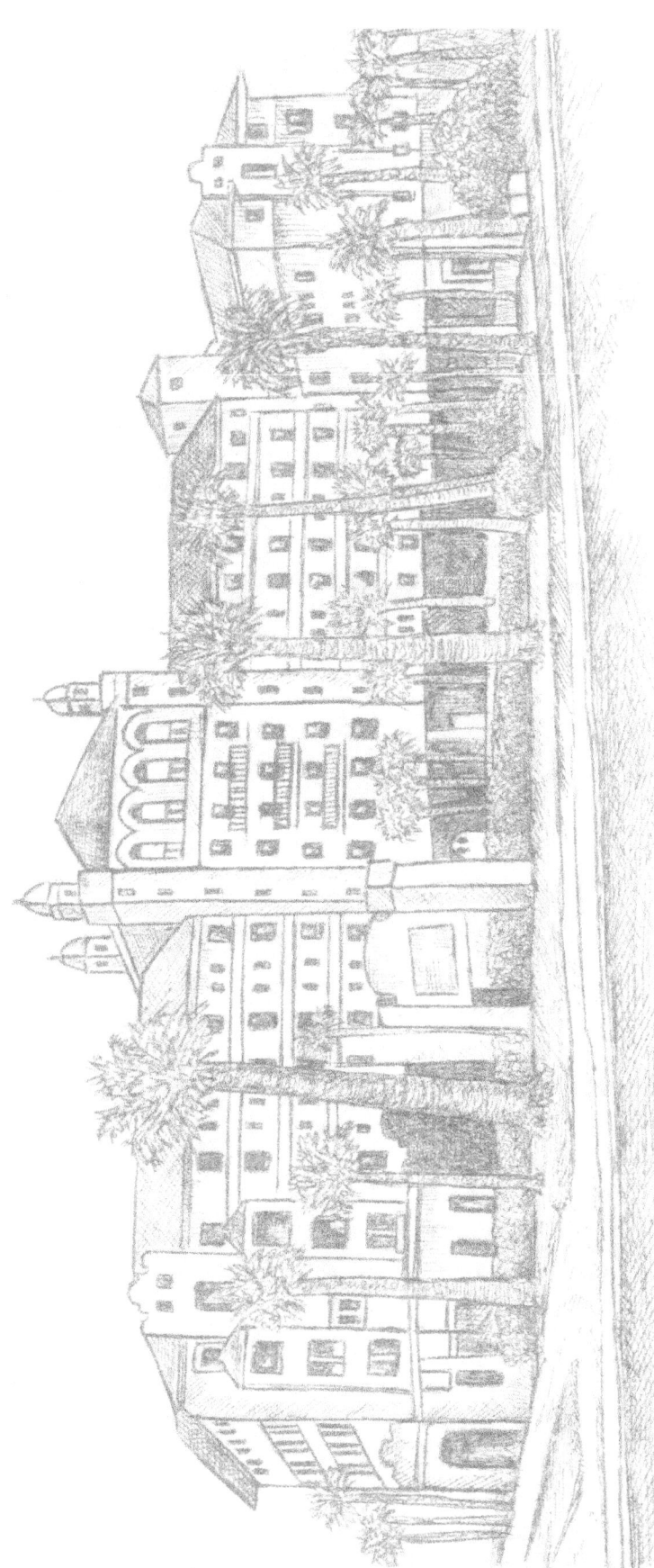

Hotel Galvez

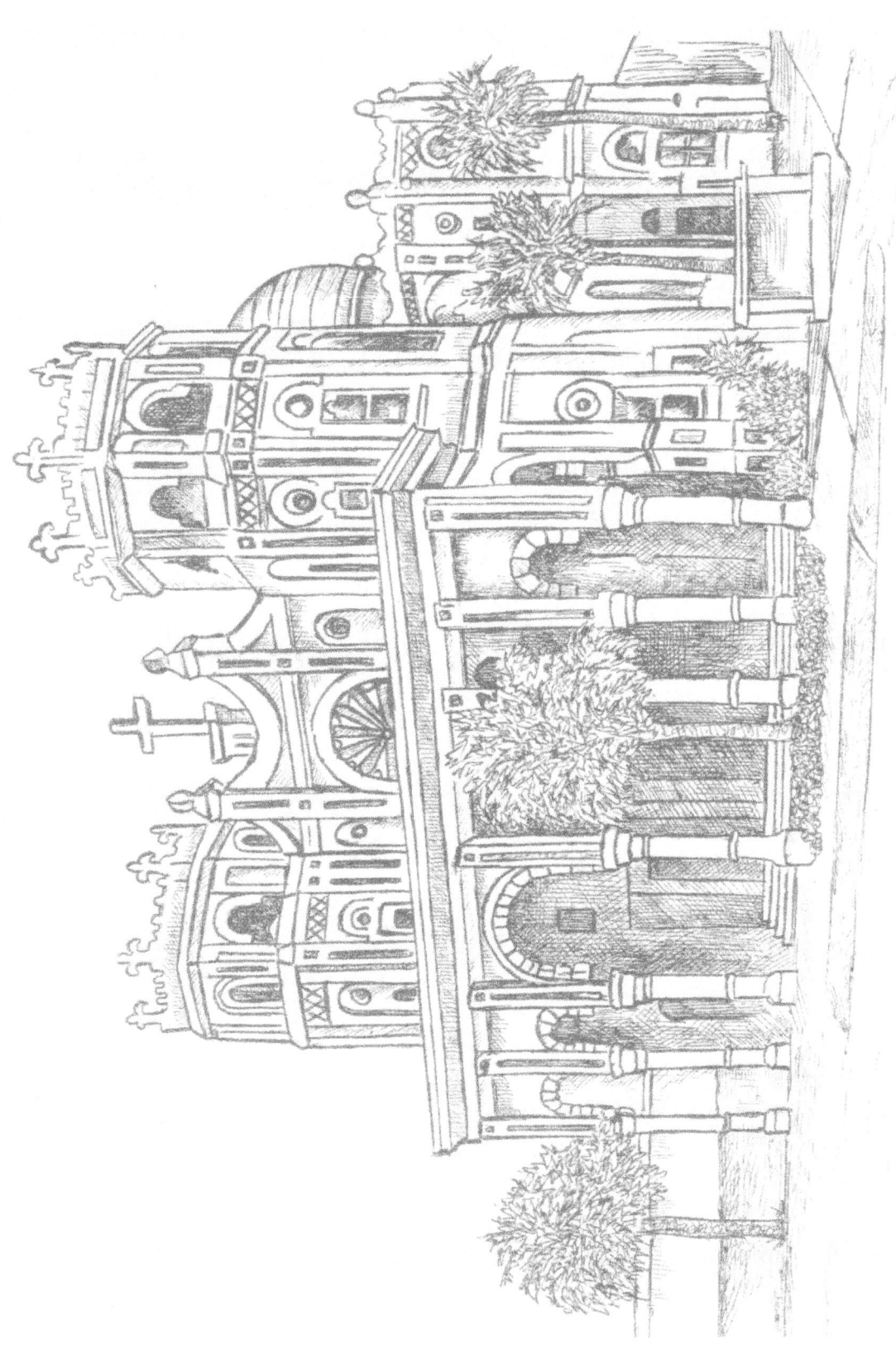

Sacred Heart Church

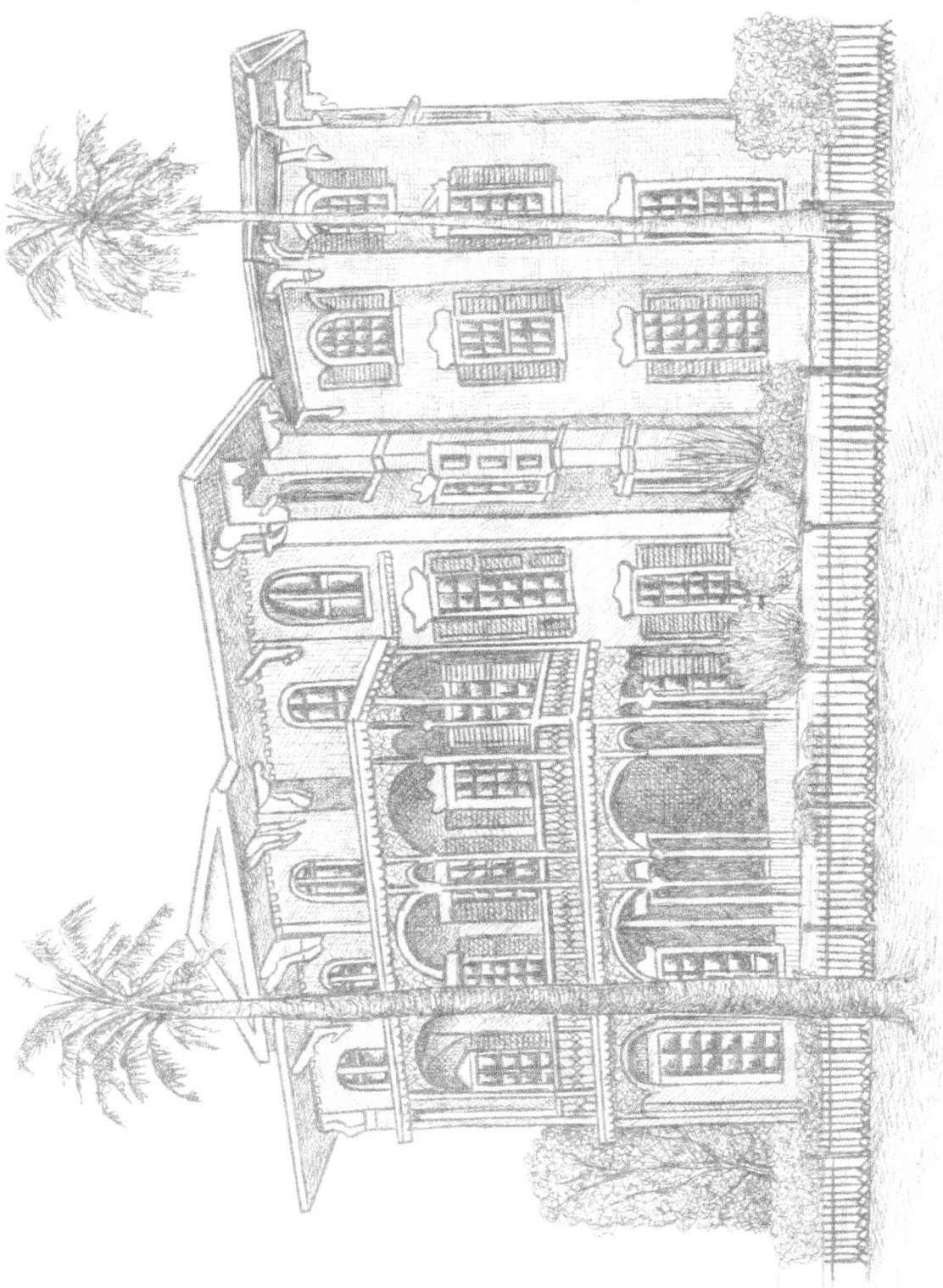

Ashton Villa

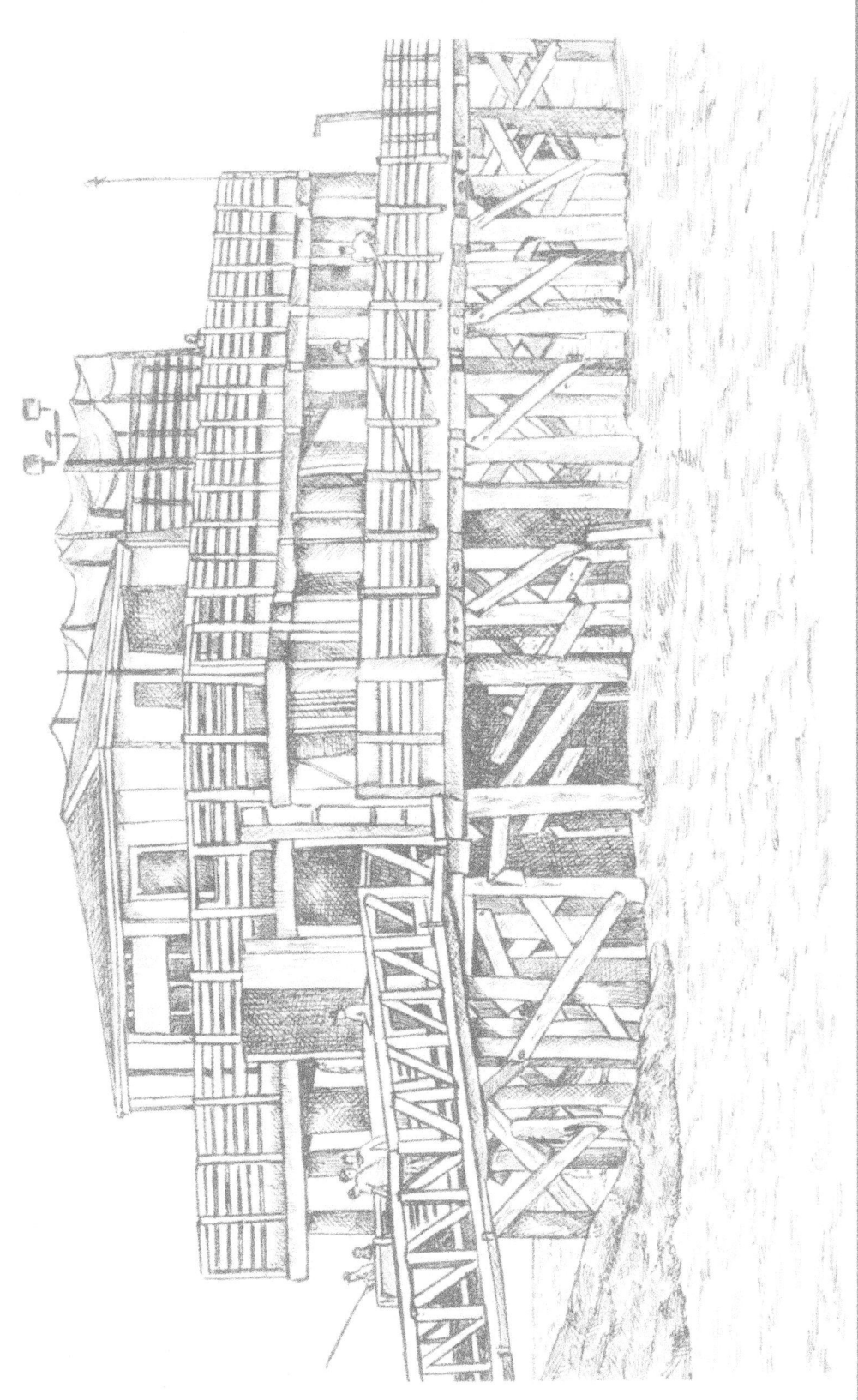

61st Street Pier

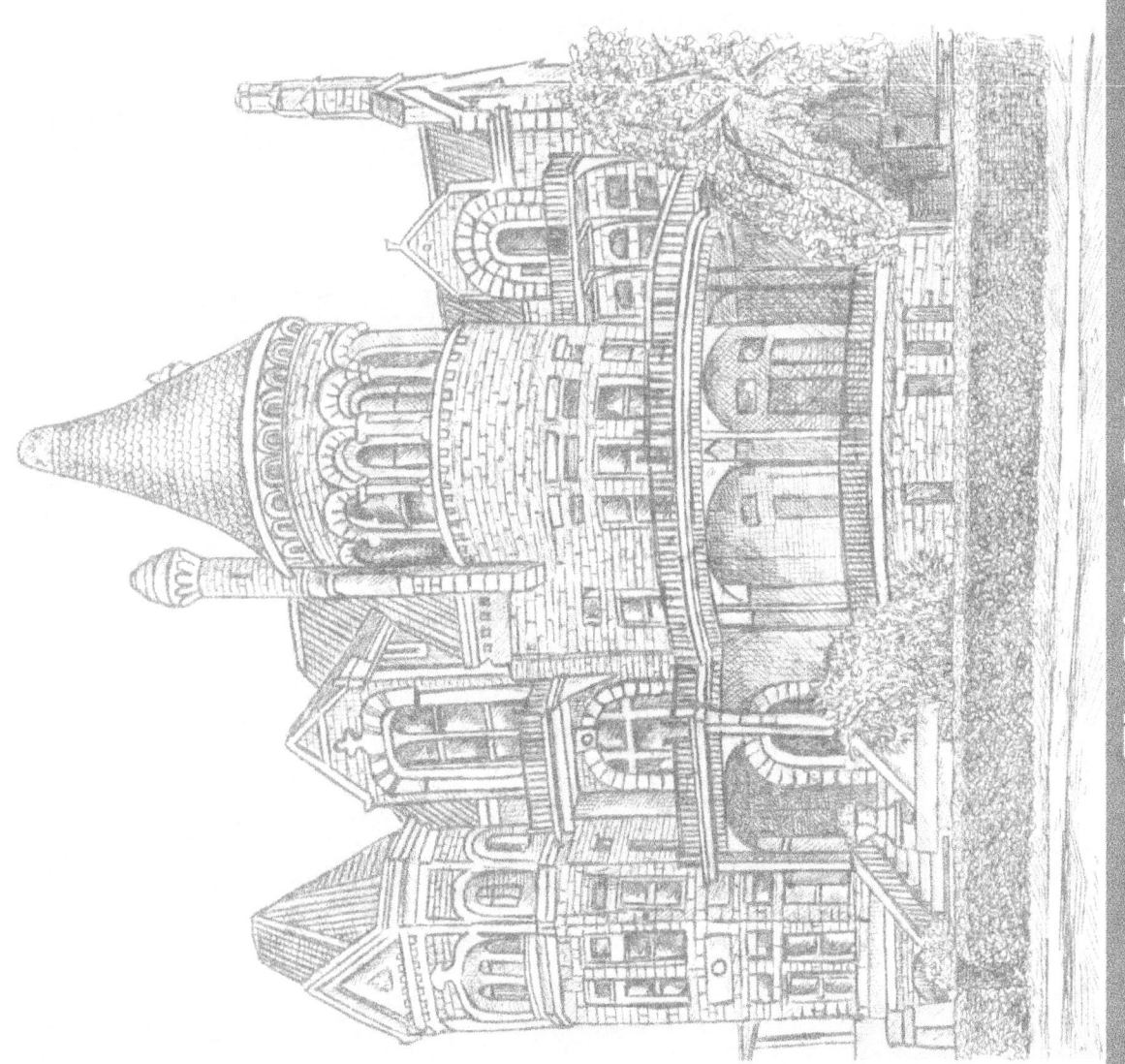

The Bishop's Palace

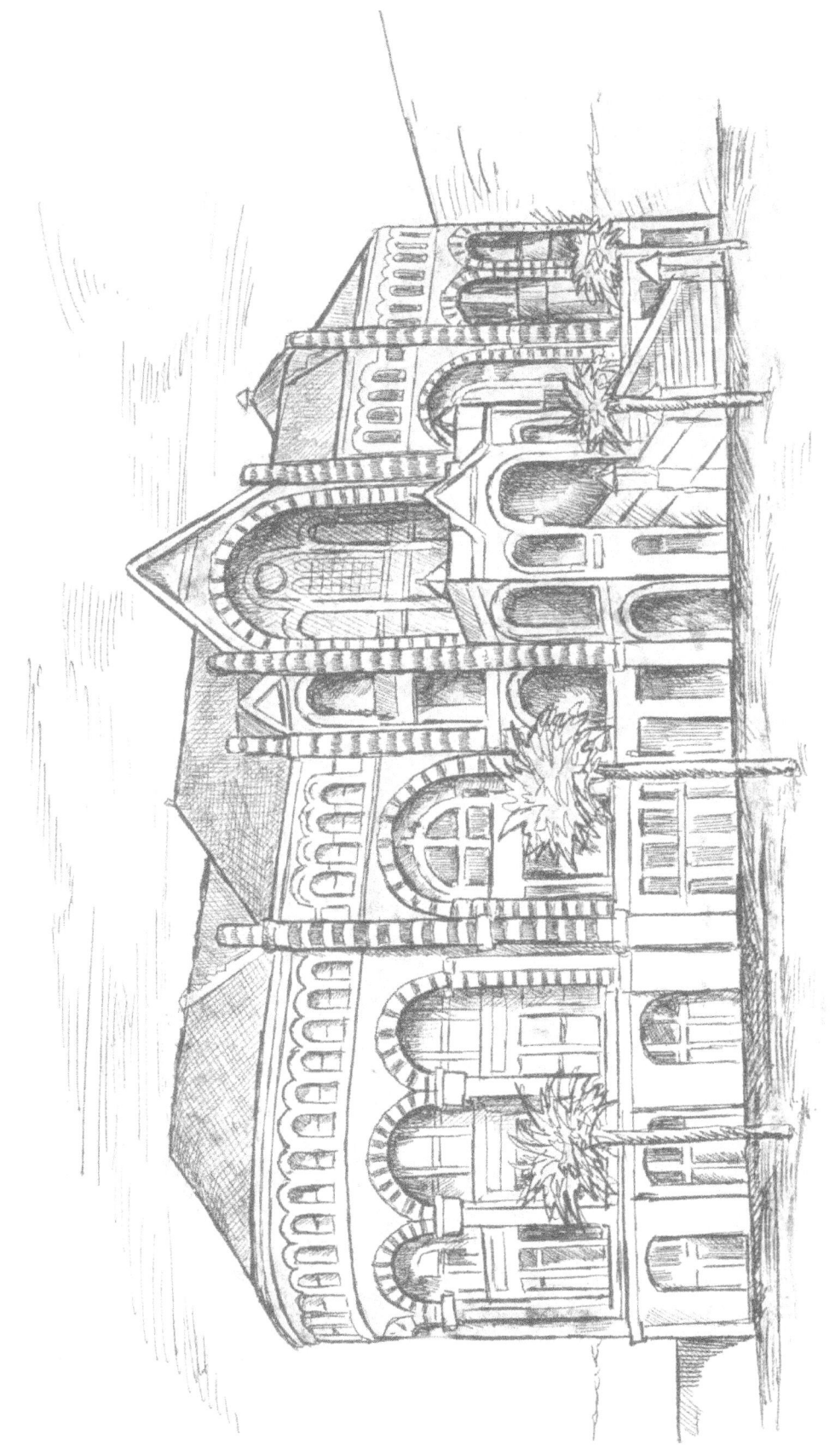

Old Red - UTMB

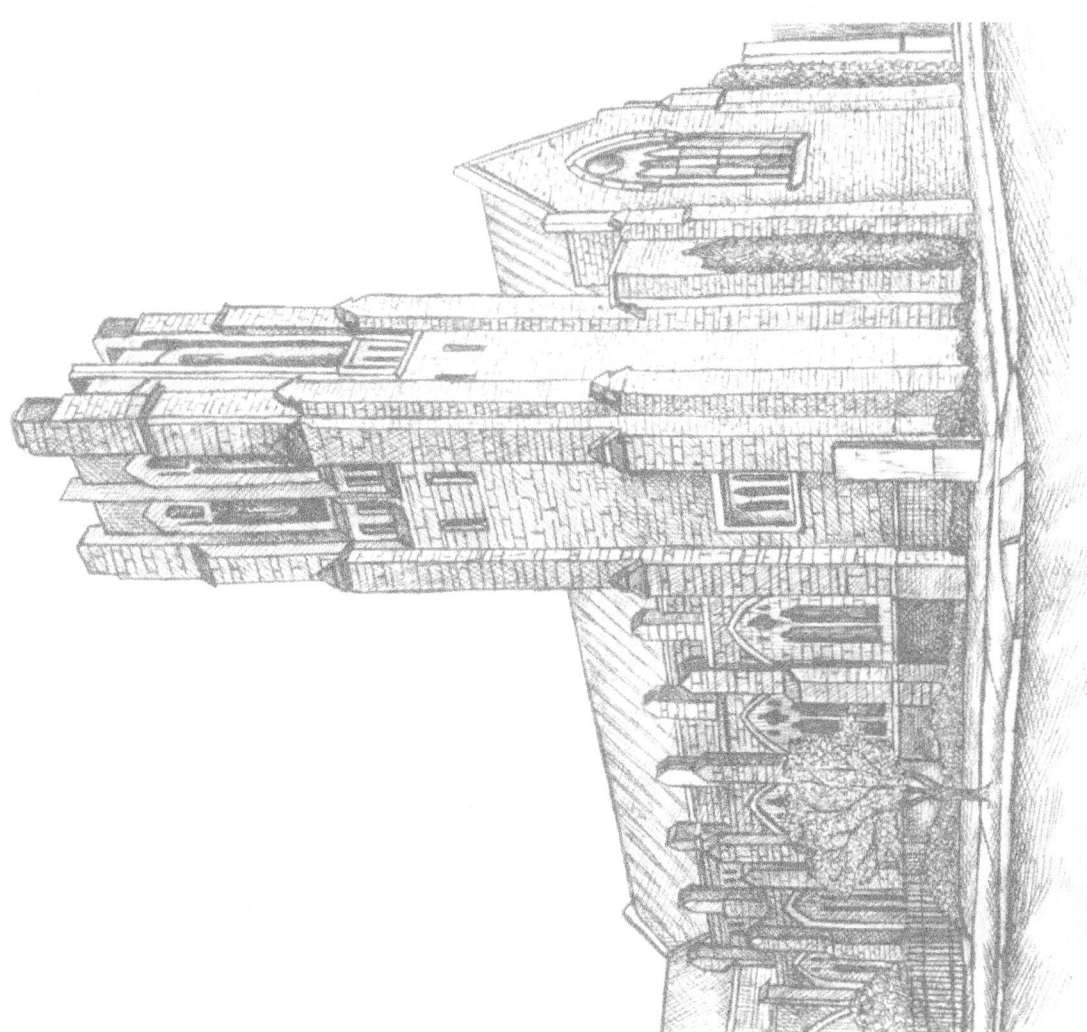

First Evangelical Lutheran Church

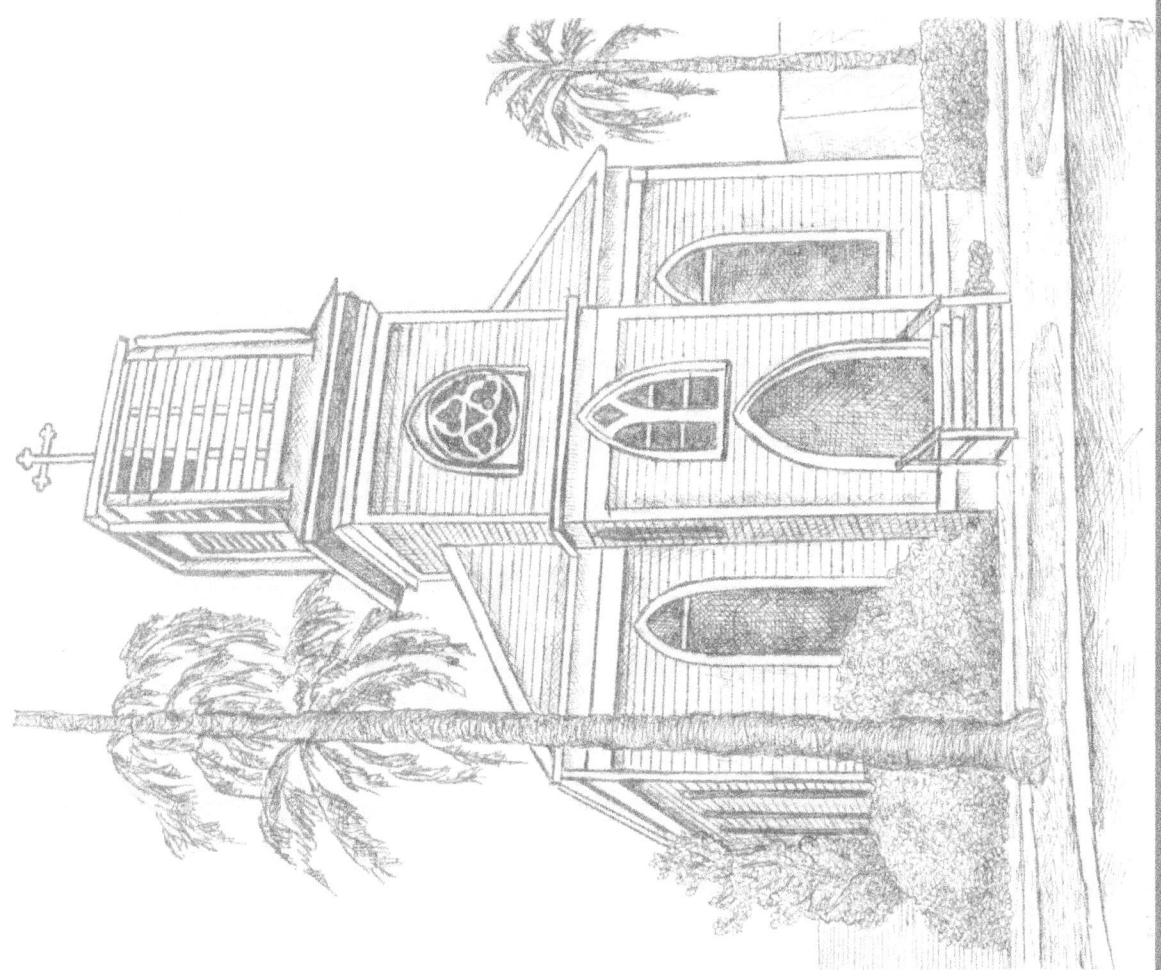

St. Joseph's Church

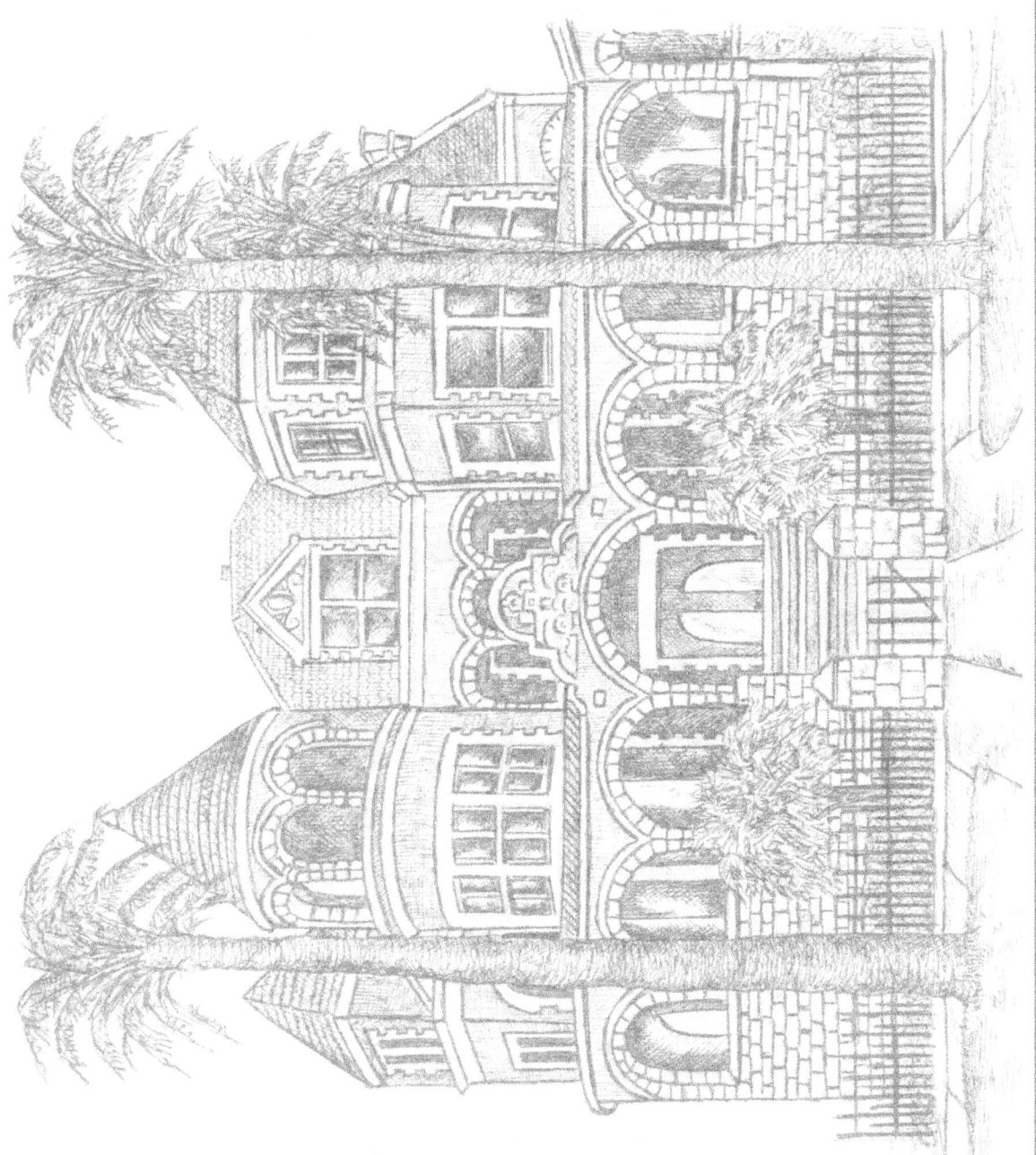

Moody Mansion

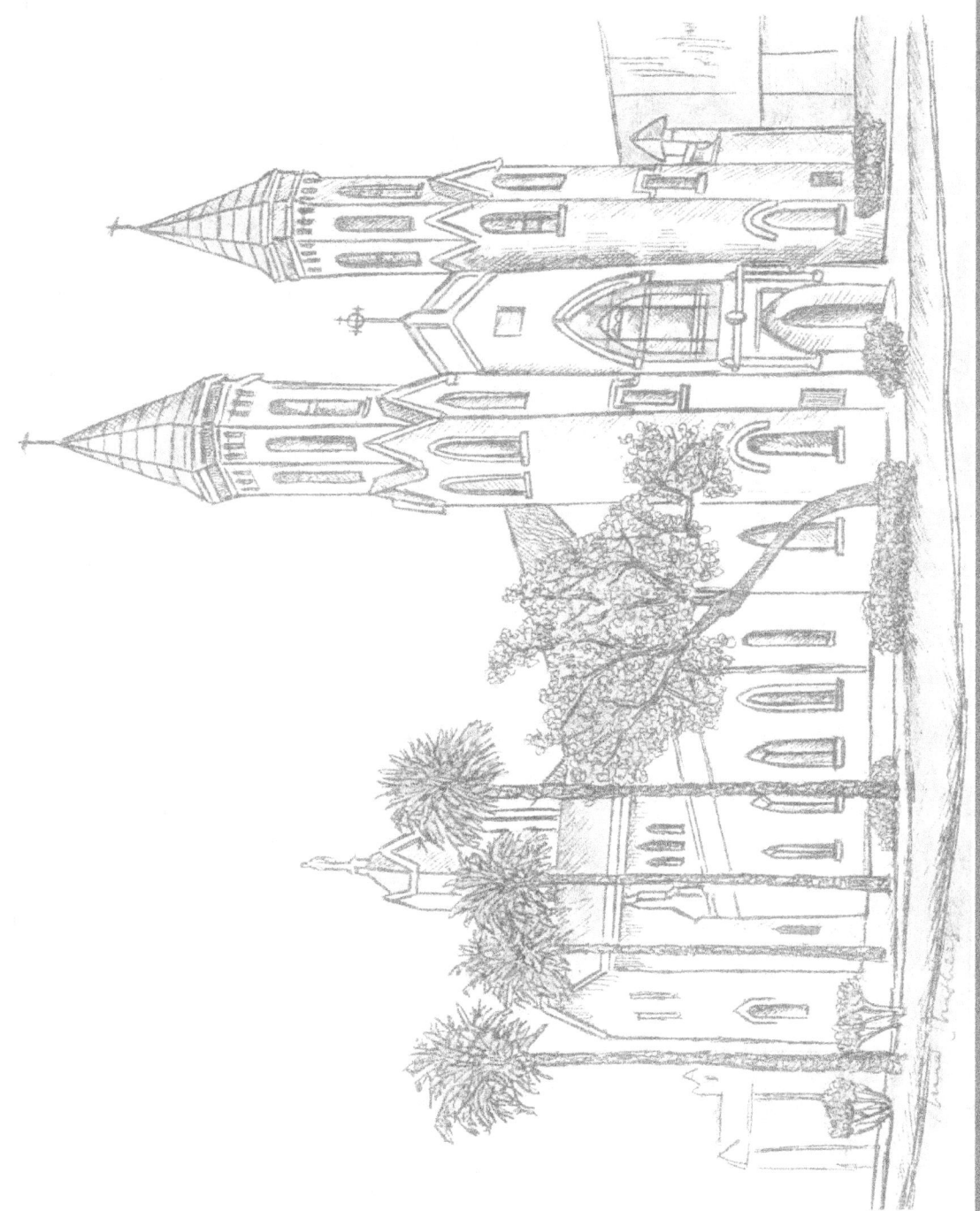

St. Mary's Cathedral

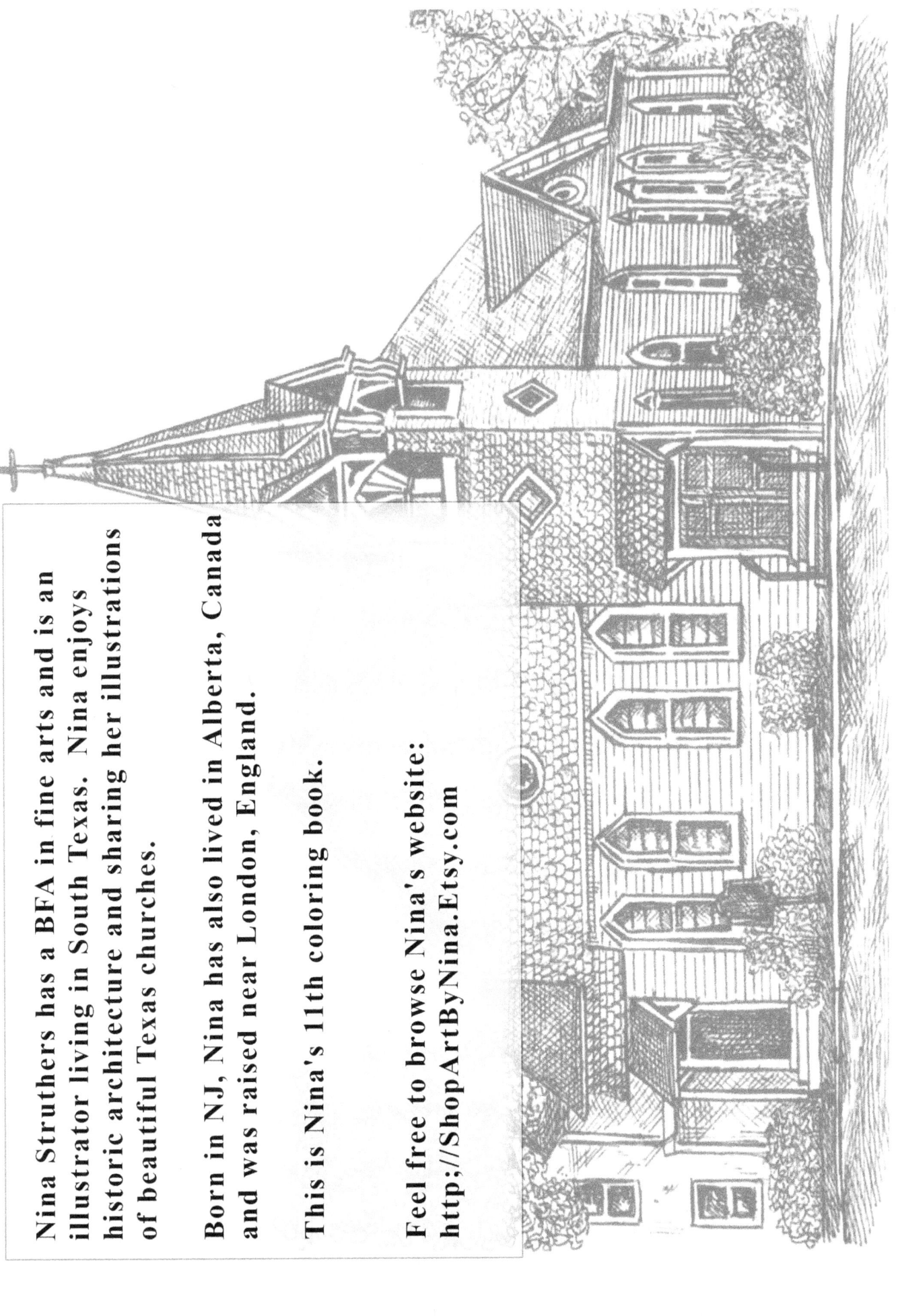

Nina Struthers has a BFA in fine arts and is an illustrator living in South Texas. Nina enjoys historic architecture and sharing her illustrations of beautiful Texas churches.

Born in NJ, Nina has also lived in Alberta, Canada and was raised near London, England.

This is Nina's 11th coloring book.

Feel free to browse Nina's website:
http://ShopArtByNina.Etsy.com